JOBS, WOMEN AND SLAVES

Colonial America History Book 5ᵗʰ Grade
Children's American History

In this book, we're going to talk about the jobs that women and slaves had in Colonial America. So, let's get right to it!

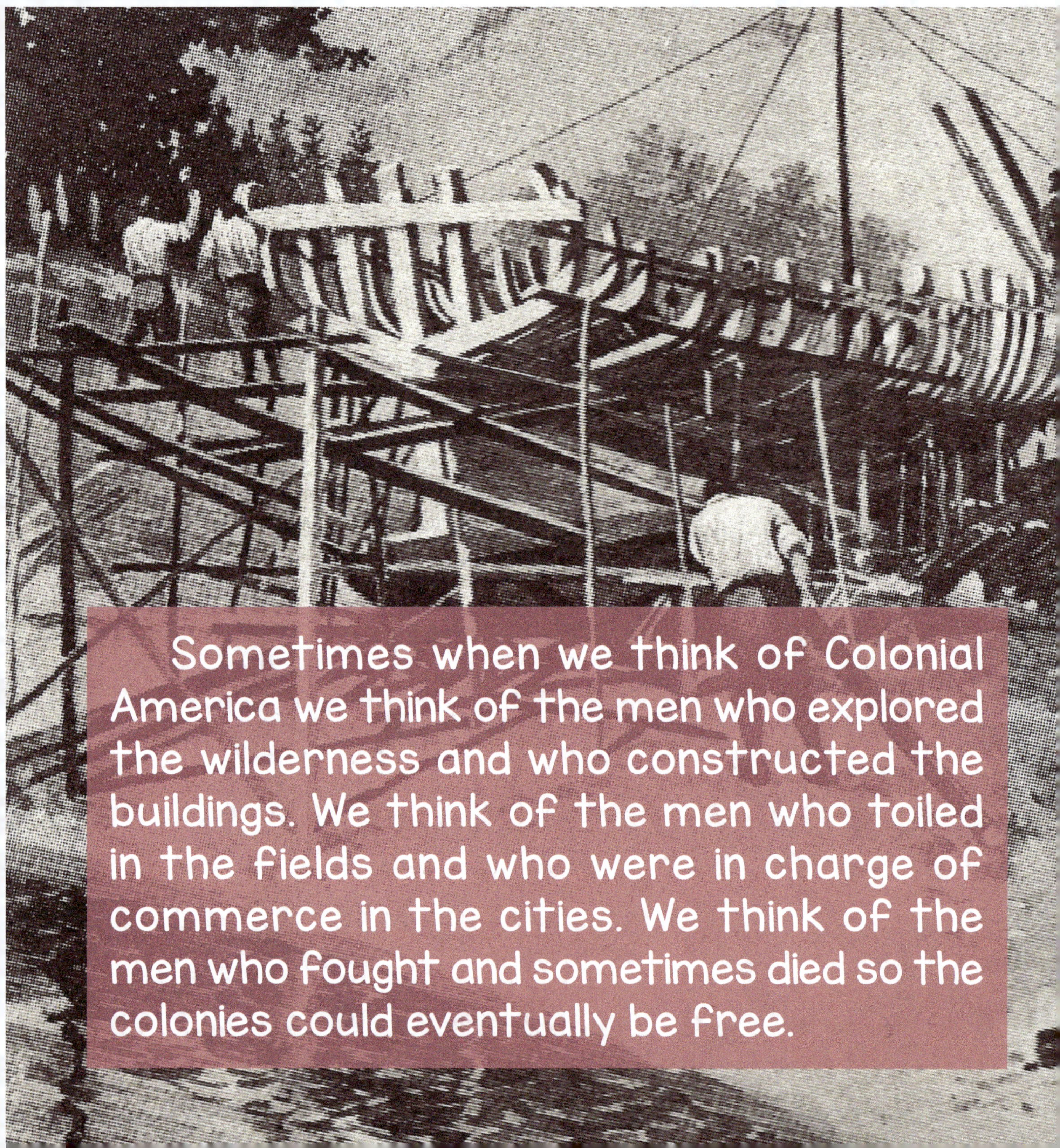

Sometimes when we think of Colonial America we think of the men who explored the wilderness and who constructed the buildings. We think of the men who toiled in the fields and who were in charge of commerce in the cities. We think of the men who fought and sometimes died so the colonies could eventually be free.

Early American colonial shipbuilders constructing
their own ship by the water

However, the men couldn't have done any of these things if they didn't have help from two important groups—women and slaves.

JOBS WOMEN PERFORMED IN COLONIAL TIMES

Women work hard today, but for the most part, their work isn't as physically demanding as it was in colonial times. Women in colonial times had a life that was sometimes very harsh. They didn't have many rights. They were rarely allowed the opportunity to read, write, or learn.

They were expected to support and obey the men in the household. They couldn't make their own decisions about anything that they did. They gave birth to the children, sometimes without a doctor or midwife in attendance. Most colonial women had nine children or more during their childbearing years. Many of the children didn't reach adulthood. The women raised and took care of the children. In addition, they were responsible for managing everything in the home.

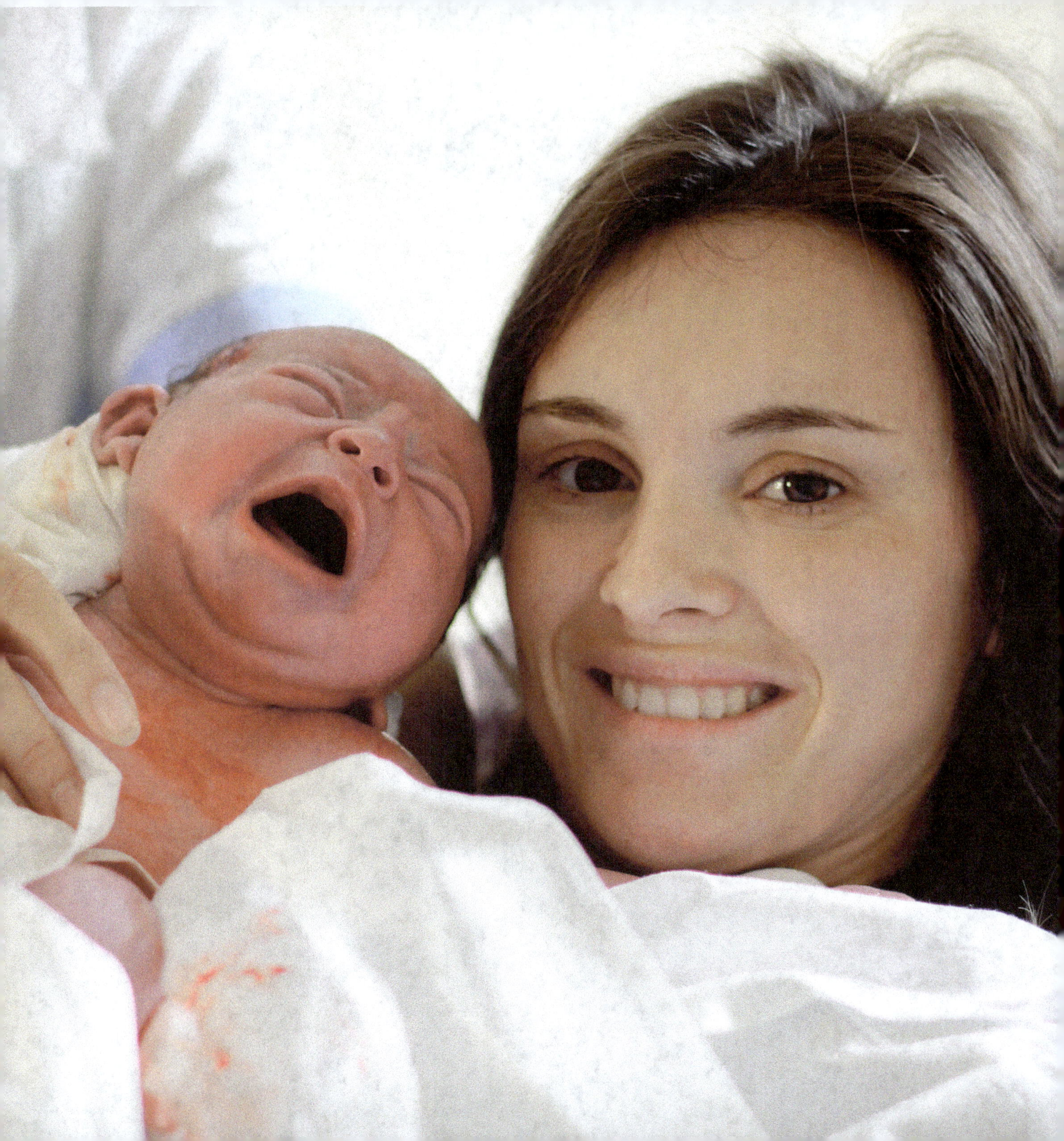

MEAL PREPARATION

The women also cooked all the meals. Perhaps this doesn't seem too difficult, but in those days there was no refrigeration or convenience foods that were prepared in advance. There were no microwave ovens. Colonial women generally cooked all the food in a big pot that was suspended in the fireplace. Everything that they made had to be cooked from scratch.

In fact, most of the day was spent preparing and cleaning up after meals. They had to maintain the fire in the kitchen, carry water from an outdoor pump or well to indoors, gather fresh fruits and vegetables, and bring in meat where it was stored in the smokehouse. All of these tasks had to done before breakfast was even prepared!

Starting and keeping a fire going was a lot of work, so the women rarely let the fire go out completely. There were usually some burning embers from the night before. Once the fire was rekindled, the breakfast meal was prepared. Mush mixed with some milk and a little molasses for sweetness was usually the breakfast meal.

Burning embers

The meal in the middle of the day was called dinner and was usually a stew made from meats and vegetables of the season. The midday meal was the biggest meal of the day and was put on the table between noon and three o'clock in the afternoon. The stew was kept edible for a span of a few days by placing it in the back area of the hearth so it would stay on a very low simmer.

Stew

Since that same stew was eaten for the evening meal, the housewife might freshen it up with some additional vegetables or herbs. Sometimes as a special treat, the housewife might prepare a pudding treat for the children, which was steamed in a fabric bag over the pot.

As if this wasn't strenuous enough, the cookware in those days was enormous. Women had to be very strong to lift kettles that were made of brass or copper and held fifteen gallons of stew. Some of the iron pots they used weighed upwards of forty pounds.

In addition to preparing the daily foods, women spent a lot of time preserving fruits and also vegetables for use during the winter months. Most housewives tended their own gardens as well.

Woman making candle

SOAP AND CANDLE MAKING

The home goods that we buy off the shelf in our modern stores were all handmade by women in colonial times. In the autumn, colonial women made candles for use throughout the year. It was incredibly hard work to make homemade candles.

They made them by dipping a set of candle rods repeatedly. These candle rods had rows of hanging wicks. The wicks went into boiling water in huge iron kettles and then in tallow that was melted. The tallow was fat from sheep or cattle. The job was hot, smelly, and incredibly tiresome. Most women didn't look forward to the autumn candle-making season.

Ashes

Women made soap too. They made it from animal fat that was leftover combined with lye. Women saved grease and the ashes from burning wood to make the abrasive lye. To make a barrel of good quality soap, they needed lots of ashes, about six bushels. They also needed lots of grease—over 20 pounds of it.

The grease and the lye mixture had to be boiled outside over an outdoor fire because it smelled so bad. It took a lot of stirring. Sometimes the soap was successful and sometimes it wasn't. Clothes were washed by hand once a month.

WEAVING AND SEWING

As if women didn't have enough to do, the other task that fell upon them was to spin, weave, and dye cloth as well as to create thread. All these things had to be done before garments could be created for the family.

Flax was grown as a crop on the farm. It was planted in the fields during the month of May. It was a quick-growing plant and was harvested at the end of June. The fibers of the plant were spun by women using a spinning wheel.

Flax sheaf drying on a field

Linen thread

The end product was linen thread that could be woven into cloth for bedding as well as clothing. There were some women who became experts at spinning and never married. It became their full-time job. This is where the term "spinster" came from.

Eventually women figured out that the tasks of creating fabric and clothing from start to finish could be done together instead of in isolation. They got together with other women in events called "bees" to do their sewing and socialize.

Women sewing

Women had a very difficult life in Colonial America. They toiled from dawn to sundown every day. However, without the women's hard work, colonial men would never have been able to succeed in building the colonies and creating a new life in America.

JOBS PERFORMED BY SLAVES IN COLONIAL TIMES

When the colonies first started, the first slaves were indentured servants. They were shipped to America from Britain and it was understood that they would be laborers. Some of these people had chosen to work for seven years so they could come to the New World. Others had massive debts or had committed crimes and this was their way of "serving their time."

    The first Africans who came to Virginia as indentured servants arrived in 1619. Most of these first servants were given their freedom after their seven years of time.

    As the population of the colonies increased, it was more and more difficult to obtain indentured servants. This was the time period when servants became slaves and weren't able to win their freedom. By the end of the 1600s, it was common for landowners to have slaves that they owned like property. In the 1700s, new legislation was passed in the colonies that specified the so-called "legal" rights of landowners to own slaves. Slaves had no rights and had to perform tasks as their masters commanded.

Slaves performed many different types of jobs, especially jobs that involved demanding physical labor. In the northern colonies, slaves worked on farms, in the cities, and on ships.

In the South, they were typically field hands. They worked a steady fifteen hours a day where they helped raise the crops, herd the livestock, and slaughter animals. The southern plantations generally had crops of cotton, rice, or tobacco. It wasn't unusual for slaves on cotton plantations to be commanded to pick 250 pounds of cotton every day. They were whipped severely if they didn't perform.

Sometimes slaves were asked to work in the master's house. These slaves were skilled laborers who knew how to keep a household running smoothly. It was considered to be an honor to serve the master and his family.

Family and slave house servants

Although some masters treated their slaves well, many others treated their slaves with extreme cruelty. Slaves had no rights and had to do whatever their masters requested 24 hours a day, 7 days a week. Their lives were filled with both physical and mental suffering. They could be bought or sold just like objects at any time. When their children got old enough they were sold and send away. Sometimes the members of a family never got to see each other again.

Branding slaves

Women slaves had the most difficult lives of all these groups in colonial society. Slave women often worked long days in the fields and then came home to take care of their own households. They raised their children knowing that they would be taken away and would become slaves as well. It was a very sad, difficult life.

SUMMARY

Women had few rights and slaves had no rights in colonial society. Women slaves probably had the most difficult life of all. The work that women and slaves had to do was extremely difficult and for the most part their lives were harsh and filled with suffering. However, without their dedication and hard work, the colonies would most likely have never survived and the United States of America wouldn't exist today.

Now that you know more about the jobs women and slaves had in Colonial America, you may want to read about the strange time period when women were accused of being witches in the Baby Professor book The Salem Witch Trials - History 5th Grade.

Visit
BABY PROFESSOR
EDUCATION KIDS
www.BabyProfessorBooks.com
to download Free Baby Professor eBooks
and view our catalog of new and exciting
Children's Books

9 7 9 8 8 6 9 4 3 5 2 9 3